Echoes of a Voice Once Heard

The Writings of RJ Corradino

When we speak,
I want my words to gently
Fall against your heart,
Letting slip the latches
To your mind.

This book is being published in loving memory of our son RJ. He was an enormously talented young man as well as being a very caring and loving person. We were so blessed to have had him in our lives and there is no doubt that we learned much more from him than he ever learned from us.

This book is dedicated to all those individuals who are living with disabilities, especially those affected by Spinal Muscular Atrophy.

All proceeds from this book will be donated to Cure SMA an organization that is working towards a cure for SMA and provides support for SMA patients and their families. Anyone wishing to make an additional donation can send it to Cure SMA, 925 Busse Road, Elk Grove Village, IL 60007.

Echoes of a Voice
Once Heard

Edited by:

Holly Corradino
&
Christina Major

Cover art by:
christina j. corradino, artist

Acknowledgements

We'd like to extend a special thanks to the following people: Steve and Michelle Wilson for their invaluable advice and input throughout this process. Dolph Corradino for the idea for the book's title and his constant encouragement. Also thanks to all those who added their thoughts and memories of RJ to make this book complete.

RJ Corradino wrote, "I don't think writing is about power. I don't feel a desire to create or destroy. My desire is for connections. I write to form connections with people. That's all." Throughout the lines of his poetry, RJ weaves the struggles we endure throughout our life along with life's celebrations. We do indeed connect with the timeless messages portrayed in RJ's poetry.

As a student at Richard Stockton College, RJ studied Literature and Creative writing under Pulitzer Prize winning poet Stephen Dunn until his untimely death at the age of twenty. Despite his disability and wheelchair dependence, RJ maintained a loving spirit, a sense of humor and a quiet dignity. His poetry lives on as a tribute to his memory.

~~~~

Among the many reasons why people loved him was that in his wheelchair, with his physical difficulties, RJ never attempted to elicit pity. He asked merely to be taken as he was-an interesting young man who shared your interests. I can't say that I loved him (I try not to love my students), but I admired his intelligence, good humor, and most of all his dignity. At the time of his death he was writing indeed some very moving poetry. In particular, a love poetry that attested to his imagination as much as it did to his desires.

Though it's doubtful that RJ had experienced carnal love (I hope he did), he certainly experienced it in his poems. And he also certainly had his dream woman who doubled as his muse; many of his poems are directed to her. In my favorite poem of his, "Cancer's Proposal", he says, I am I. I've nothing more or less to be but this body (strange as it is beautiful, beautiful as it is amusing) and proceeds to say to her that, although his hands are like claws, he has "eyes ... that can embrace you". Of course as he's offering her this, he's offering her more: a lovely sensibility, a good mind, a burgeoning talent. That's what he offered us as well.

Stephen Dunn 2002

Fabric Moments
The Words of RJ Corradino

Gateway to Honesty

My God, I'm terrible about keeping a journal. I know. It's really strange because I feel like I do more thinking and reading about journals than I do actually writing in one. I read and ponder every freewriting technique of every kind. I download programs, play with them, get set up for myself, write a first entry --

and never touch it again. Silly isn't the word for it, it's downright ludicrous.

But I know why I have this problem. I think I know, at any rate. I used to think it was that it felt meaningless --"Like writing a letter to nobody" was what I called it in the first journal I never wrote in. But that isn't it.

It's the honesty of it. When I write here, I am forced to assess my life, my mindset, my thoughts, my person. I can't lie here -- because I'm writing this for me. I can't bullshit me. I know me too well.

I wish I could put on paper how odd I feel right now (if I was a good poet, I'd be able to). This isn't all that comfortable. I have been squirming from the very first paragraph. A part of me would love to close this program right now, and run out of the room. But, I'm still here.

:pause:

I'm here because it feels good, in-some strange way. This assessment, self-therapy, whatever. I think I always knew about that concept -- releasing emotion through art -- and I think I always thought I was doing it. Maybe I was at certain odd moments. But this is the first time I'm feeling a real, strong outflow.

Sometimes I feel like I'm just beginning to become a writer. That's silly -- I started writing in grade 8. But the things I wrote then didn't matter to me. Not like what I write now. It's easy to say that -- it probably isn't true.

I really wasn't writing consistently until now. I have a lot of poems, essays and things that I wrote these past few months; but to give you anything earlier I'd need to stretch back 4 years or so. It's like I've been pretending to be a writer all that time.

I was going to say that I feel like I'm writing well, suddenly, in comparison to my earlier work. But that's unfair. Of course, I'm a better writer now than I was four years ago. And I'm sure I'm not as good a writer as I will be 2, 4, 10 years from now. My style will change and improve as time passes, I'm sure of that.

~~~~

A poem I wrote in high school;

The Vastness of Time and Space

When I look at you,
I see the vastness of time and space,
And I thank you graciously
For showing me your power.
And now I see
That under your command:
Mountains will migrate far across a continent
Only to crumble to dust
And sink into the sea.
Great empires will arise
Only to one day fall
And be forever forgotten.

Oceans will boil
Until the earth is
Completely barren of moisture.

The dead will crawl forth
From their prisons
Six feet below the ground
And walk among the living.

The sun will turn black
And as cold as the ground we walk on,
Petrified,
Completely quenched of it's

Godlike flame.

And the moon will
Burst into mighty fire,
Like a great phoenix.

My family loved this, and I was so proud of it. But as I reread it now, I'm not sure I like it very much. It's powerful sounding, but it doesn't mean a whole lot when I read it now.

It's too grandiose. It isn't about God, as a lot of people suspect. If my memory serves me well, the poem is about me, as egotistical as that may seem. It's about the powers I had, or thought I should have, being a writer.

But for me - here, now - I don't think writing is about power. At all. I don't feel a desire to create or destroy (maybe this is why I no longer write fiction). My desire is for connections. I write to form connections with people. That's all.

I wrote this a few weeks ago:

When we speak,
I want my words to gently
fall against your heart,
letting slip the latches
to your mind.

This is closer to my true mindset, here and now. It is short, simple, and clear. And it's honest. I promise I will write more here. Soon.

Conversing

So much exchanged:
between two pairs of soft eyes;
the stillness of his body, on the bed;
the gentle breeze from her nude form;
in each step of her evening ritual --
hairbrush, shower curtain, steam, silk nightgown;
in her giggle,
in the sock she throws, as she catches him spying yet again;
in his sheepish, blushing smirk.

So many words within:
the swish of the top sheet pulled aside;
the rumble of the mattress as she lays with him,
rolling slowly, her hand crossing over his chest
to scratch his face, resting her chin near his neck,
resting her lips in the space behind his ear;
the kisses,
the hisses, the thumps of slow breaths and heartbeats;
the slight crack as he opens his mouth, words searching for exit;
the single finger, laid upon his lips;
the kissing, the gentle nibbling of her hand;
the unspoken, redundant word.

Such a pleasant conversation they had, as they closed their eyes
and drifted, lingering one step above sleep.

~~~~

Alone,
he sleeps as a terrified child
clutching at his
moist cocoon
of knotted sheets
and strained bed pillows.

Nightclub observations
Club Extasia, circa 2012

Red lights exploded;
pulsed, throbbed,
burned their way

across the unholy
crowd of creatures.

I saw a boy
with wide eyes
and a girl
with pixie hair.
Their faces held onto innocence,
their bodies slithered across one another
in robotic bliss

Soon she put a drop of magic liquid on her tongue.
Her thin, sexy blue lips
reached out, crossing his mouth;
they shared the synthetic beauty.
A bass tone exploded;
pulsed, throbbed,
rippled

across the unholy
crowd of creatures.

Shaken,
frightened by things
deeper than the low reverberations,
I lost my balance and
fell into you.

Your knees were as weak as my own
and, in feeling this,
we melted into the heavy weeping bass.

We vibrated together
for a moment of living beauty,
and then were separated --
{someone bumped into you or I, and}
we returned to our own private nightmares.

On an Outing with My Son

I took him to the park last week.
Giving him a coin,
I let him step away from my wheelchair
striding to the pond's edge.
Eyes shut,
face in a knot,
he tossed the silver piece with dignity.

I pulled him to my lap,
hugging him
as tightly as my bony arms could grasp.
We sat together and watched his wish
sink into the murky bottom.
With a dream, a veil
clouding his tiny face,
he told me "Daddy,
I wished for you to walk someday."

I froze.

I thought of my youth:
Such faith I had in destiny,
God's loving plan
of endless earthly lessons.

I knew,
or used to know
that overcoming a true burden
meant first resigning to it.

Must this be the day I taught my child the art of giving up?

Confusion, terror filled my heart.
Those wondering eyes
that looked to me
were somehow wiser than my own.

I knew nothing that a father ought to know.
I muttered in my mind a prayer,
thanking God for my son's thoughtfulness
and wishing his faith would linger longer than my own.

~~~~

Alone in the kitchen,
her skin parted at the mercy of the broken wine glass;

His hands and hers. That is all there is.
Large fingers; careful, gentle.

Moments as this are rare and crucial.
The party,
the dancers,
the noise fading to a blurry calm,
drifting with the endless moments
leading up to now, to here;
drifting with the vast questions of the future.

She could feel,
touch the moment,
sense it in his fingers,
in his caress,
a clumsy grace
removing the shard from her hand.

Bactine and a Band-Aid on her wound,
she dreamily swept the mess
into the dustpan...

~~~~

Sunshower

On this sharp, crisp day of spring
we were startled as the first cool splash of water hit your face
and rolled from your forehead, down across your nose's bridge,
resting with a smirk beneath your lip. I kissed it away.
We laughed - running, spinning

as flowers; we enjoyed the feel of joy-infused droplets
springing from our skin,
embracing the brilliant-colored fiber
of our clothes, our hair.

In that sunny rain, bathed in liquid color,
you shimmered with the radiance of the day we met.

~~~~

This is stillness:

as rain seeps
from dim stars,
laughing against
closed windows;

as night wind threatens
door latches;

as the fan whispers
bittersweet, cold silence;

I turn
over
brittle pages
of this journal,

writing nothing.

Tributes

Dear Family and Friends

It has been said!

"That a person is not dead while their name is still spoken. That we are only truly gone when we disappear from the memories of those who loved us."

Monday March 30th was the 20th Anniversary of our son RJ's passing. Holly and I have been working on putting together a memorial book, which we will self-publish, that will include many of his Poems and Essays. The work we have done will soon be completed and we thought that we would give each of you an opportunity to be part of it. We know that RJ was either influenced, touched or had been part of your life in some way. Because of that connection, we thought it would be great if you would care to lend a word, a thought or a memory that we can make part of this book. Our goal is to get the book out by July 20th which also happens to be his birthday.

To me RJ was not only a loving nephew and talented writer but an "Inspiration". Along with a wonderful sense of humor, he was an example of patience, fortitude, gentleness, thoughtfulness and a loving spirit. I feel so privileged to have had him in my life. When he died, he took with him a part of my heart.

Love,
Aunt Nikki

When I take my walks on beautiful days I look up to the sun and sky and you are the first person I sense. This awakens feelings in me much different than thoughts of other loved ones who have left us, perhaps because there was much unsaid between you and me. You know what my thoughts are and how your life affected me. I have kept and treasured your books of poetry, a file of writings and articles from people who wrote about you. Your imaginative, compassionate, and sensitive style of expression resonated with all who were lucky enough to know and love you. When I read again an article that Shaun Reilly, assistant editor of Argo, wrote after your passing, I am very aware that I missed a lot. I am honored to have this collection of your writings and grateful that your mom and dad put this book together. Watch me, as I continue to "Look Up" to you!

Love you,
Aunt Joan

I never heard RJ complain, but I always heard him laugh. At family get togethers, he would be playing with his cousins. Whether they were playing a computer game or just hanging out, he was always laughing. RJ got so much joy out of being with Michael and Ashley and with Jon and Steve. I could always find them by their laughter. Randy, especially could get RJ laughing so hard he cried. Randy would make up some ridiculous story or make faces and it never failed to make RJ laugh. His sense of humor was infectious. I always left his company in a better mood and frame of mind.

Love,
Uncle Barry

R. J. Corradino -

My memories go back to happy days over happy weekends when R.J. would spend countless hours playing with my kids, Michael and Ashley. Michael and R.J. would assemble elaborate Lego structures while Ashley would roam around with Sparky, the dog, who was almost as big as she was. They would play for hours on end, only appearing occasionally when forced to come to dinner or get ready for bed - definitely their least favorite time. Though I miss R.J. with all my heart, memories like this bring a smile to my face and comfort to my heart.

Love, Aunt Amy

In the 21st Century, with a few clicks of the mouse, you can uncover a whole artistic movement – instantaneously. You can listen to the entire catalog of Bob Dylan on shuffle or download all of Henry Miller's books on a PDF. Wikipedia has entries on even the bit players of music and film that even the most thorough encyclopedias of yesteryear would have pushed aside. Countless YouTube channels will point you in the right direction, no matter how obscure the artist.

In the days prior to the internet, it required a lot of work to find cool things to listen to, read, or watch. If you were searching deeper than what the mall had to offer or what the radio fed you, you had to put the work in. This meant trips to used record stores, book stores, and flea markets in towns you never heard of. Half the time you had no idea what you were looking at, if it had a far out cover or it came from the right decade (the 1960's) it was most likely going to be cool. You had to roll the dice.

My cousin RJ was into art, music, and books just like my brother Jon and I. All three of us immersed ourselves in It. It was what we did all day. When we weren't reading, we were listening to a record and when we weren't listening to a record, we were watching a movie and when we weren't watching a movie, we were talking about movies, records and books. Me being the oldest and most mobile of three, I was on the front lines. If I found something cool I would pass it on to Jon and RJ.

If I was passing a work on to them it was because, to me, there was no question it was valuable. The artifact had been vetted and was now considered a treasure. I would hand it over with authority as If it came down from the god of thunder himself. "Read this!" "You need to hear this record!" "Watch this movie!" RJ and Jon had almost no choice. They ravenously accepted whatever I was handing over and knew they were in for a blast.

As the three of us got older, it wasn't enough to just be a spectator. We had to participate. I decided to study film, Jon got into sculpture and RJ had to write. RJ's experience was different. As you'll find in his works, his drive to write was to explore life as a visionary. He was sidelined from participating in most things, but he was astute in soaking in the world that was happening around him. His writing expresses a yearning to be ordinary.

What you are looking at now is the product of the internet age. "Publish to order books" has opened up a whole world to authors that would have a difficult time finding publishers, because of the small audience for their work. When RJ was starting out in the late 20th Century it was hard to be noticed. But RJ got noticed almost right away. He was published in a small press, almost instantly. I remember how proud we were of him. He got his name on the map! He was the first of the three of us to be noticed as an artist. However ordinary RJ yearned to be, to all of us, he was **extraordinary**.

Stephen Wilson

Randy often retells a dream that he had after RJ passed. He said he saw RJ and he was still handicapped and trying to walk. Randy was saddened, that still, he couldn't use his legs. Then RJ passes him and kicks up his heels and says, "Only kidding!" and walks away. This dream gives me insight that RJ, like his father, was a joker. I imagine he must have enjoyed, like Marielle does, playing jokes on Randy. The dream also tells me that RJ needed to be free. I hope that he knows no boundaries wherever his soul is now.

Michelle Wilson

Marielle Wilson

"Something for You"
Springsteen days and Morrison nights
Among the stars
Driving down winding sunset canyon roads
Red corvette
Top down
A million miles per hour
Sun glasses at night with hair blowing in the wind.
Alone, carefree but ever present.
Your spirit burns bright on this endless road
Infinity upon infinity till the next destination and departure is
called.
The time traveler.
A weaver of memories and dreams
The ones people write movies about.

Jon Wilson

RJ,

I've been reflecting about the times we've spent together. One feeling that I keep coming back to is the thought of you as a leader in my life. I don't have a brother, but I think you are the closest I have to an older brother. Every time we used to visit you, you would have something new to show me or tell me about, whether it be a new video game, heavy metal band, or something interesting that I didn't know about. I'm not sure anyone else is aware, but you were the one who taught me what multiplication was. You were also the one that introduced me to Motley Cru, Alice Cooper, Joe Walsh, the Doors, and so many other bands. I also remember wanting to show you stuff as I got older, to try to impress you with new music I had found. I remember a couple of times showing you something new I had discovered and you thinking it was really cool. That you liked something new I had found made me feel good. I really looked up to you, and I clearly remember that approval making my day. I wonder if you were around today, what new interesting things you would show me. I wonder what it would be like to hang out with you at this age. What things would I learn from you?

What kind of things would we talk about? What kind of jokes would you make? What kind of music would you be showing me? I would love to share with you all of the interesting things that have happened in my life. To tell you about all the new music, artwork, etc. I've discovered. To tell you about all of the interesting things I've learned browsing Wikipedia. To introduce you to my family. To hear about the interesting things you discovered. Even though you are gone, my memory of you is strong and clear. I can always stop and imagine what you would think about something, what you would say. I should do that more often. I think I can still learn from you, to get your perspective on my life and the world through my memory of you.

Love,
Michael

A Letter for RJ:
Dear RJ,

Even though I never had the honor of meeting you in life, I met you by listening to the memories of our beloved Grandma Dottie. I also met you by listening to the memories of our family members: Uncle Randy and Aunt Holly, Amy and Ashley, and my husband (your cousin Michael).

One of the most beautiful memories of your life that I heard was brought up by Grandma Dottie. I remember the day when she talked about the life that you had and how difficult it was at times. However, she also discussed memories about your inspiring poetry and your amazing intelligence. She also described the enormous strength and determination that your mother, Aunt Holly, had when she fought extensively to get you the good education that you deserved in a school that did not have the appropriate facilities to accommodate you. Those memories are so precious especially now that Grandma Dottie can no longer revive them in person. I am sure your Grandmother thought of you and prayed for you every day of her life. She mentioned it when I noticed your photo on her refrigerator, next to the photo of your Uncle Mick.

I also had the opportunity to listen to the beautiful memories and passages brought to life by your Father, Uncle Randy; specifically, about those moments when you were growing up together with your cousins, Ashley and Michael. I heard that you loved to play Legos for endless hours with Michael, and Ashley wanted to join too but she was too young at the time, so she played with your doggie most of the time.

I joined our family around 2013-2014 and slowly learned about you through memories people shared with me. Nevertheless, I realize how much I missed out on not getting to be a part of your life. Sometimes I think of your life like a sunrise, the time in the morning when the sun first appears. Sunrises are the start of a day. They are so full of beautiful light and so full of the most incredible colors that the human eye can see. According to Steven Ackerman, professor of meteorology at UW-Madison, "the colors of the sunset result from a phenomenon called scattering. Molecules and small particles in the atmosphere change the direction of light rays, causing them to scatter. Scattering affects the color of light coming from the sky, but the details are determined by the wavelength of the light and the size of the particle." As you probably experienced, during a sunrise the sun starts coming up and is low on the horizon then the sunlight travels through more of the atmosphere and leaves a full color palette in the sky. During a sunrise we can see colors like blues, violets, yellow, orange, and red. Sunrises take away the darkness. They say goodbye to the night. They mark the start of a new day. Your life was so short but so full of life. Your life was so full of amazing and unique experiences like the sunrise colors. There is a sunrise in every day; but there is not a day without a sunrise. Some of us miss seeing the brief sunrise during the early morning hours. Some of us are asleep during the sunrise. Some of us are too busy and miss seeing the sunrise. Even if someone is awake and eager to see the sunrise, if he or she does not look in the right direction of the compass point, then it might be missed. Unfortunately, I missed meeting you in person. I missed seeing your remarkable sunrise. However, I treasure the opportunity to have you in my memories. I was honored to receive the opportunity to be part of the day that you started. I became part of this day by reviving the memories of those fortunate and honored ones who met you in person. I will treasure the memories I heard. I will treasure the memories I will read in this book. I will allow them to influence my life. I will share your memories with my children, Orion and Lotus. You marked a new beginning in our family and in the life of every single person that you met. Your memory is alive amongst all of us.

I thank you for the opportunity to have you in my life.

With all my love,
Adriana M. Gil Matos

RJ Corradino was smart, had a great sense of humor, was a gifted writer, and brought joy to anyone who met him. I'm the baby of the family and, to me, RJ was the cousin I looked up to and wanted to impress, without ever actually feeling pressure that I would let him down or that he would pass judgement on my attempt to impress him. My brother Michael, RJ, and I would play board games for hours, watch movies, and stay up late telling stories. I have so many fond memories from our childhood together.

I recall being interested at a young age in the many therapies that RJ participated in when we visited, but his physical disability was not something I concentrated on. RJ had strength in his words, intellect, and his physical limitations were not at the forefront of our relationship. Concentrating on his abilities prepared me for my own life journey as our own daughter would be born with Down Syndrome. As with RJ, we always celebrate her accomplishments, and I now have an even stronger appreciation for the effort and endurance which RJ had to put forth to do things that others take for granted.

RJ lives on in all of the people who were fortunate enough to know him. He has made each one of us stronger, more worldly, patient, and empathetic. I see him in my aunt and uncle. I see him when our family is together. I see him when I play board games with my children, when I'm reminded of the nights we stayed up late, and I see him in me when I think what an impact he has had on my life and my own aspirations.

Ashley Gogoj

RJ

Ashley and I began to date in the spring of 2008. By summertime, I was introduced to Holly and Randy, Ashley's aunt and uncle, RJ's mom and dad. At one of those early visits, maybe even the first, I found myself talking with Randy on the back porch of their Point Pleasant home overlooking the river. I, of course, was trying to impress Randy who is much like a father-figure to Ashley. And I remember feeling honored that he shared stories of his son who had left them much too soon. Among many stories, Randy told me that R.J wrote poetry and that he was published. This conversation was bookended when, later in the weekend, they handed me a copy of Winds of Time which contained selected poetry by RJ.

In the years that have followed, it has been a gift to hear so many more stories of R.J and his cousins. He was clearly a wonderful son, cousin, nephew, and friend, and had a beautiful spirit. And it has been a privilege to read RJ's own words, which are a small window into who he was and what he dreamed.

I regret that my own children and I cannot know R.J. We can only know him through others. But I hope that this note serves as a testament to RJ's mom and dad that they have built a home which remembers, honors, and celebrates their son. The grief caused by losing a child must be its own, special kind of sorrow. But in the Corradino home, somehow, some way, a part of that sadness has been transformed into a love, closeness, affection, and even laughter that may not have been able to exist without it. That part of RJ continues to live on as though he is able to sit around the table with us. I'm grateful to be a part of this family and honored to be able to write this note.

Mike Gogoj

Poetry

About a Broken Compass

Such a sad device:
The arrow has pulled
so strongly against the current
that it now spins rather indecisively,
not pointed in any chosen direction.

It's shiny, anyway.

~~~~

Overexposure

This photograph makes me breathe a shiver.
My face is gone.
It seems almost a negative,
but negatives are sharp and definite.
Here, I am a blurred streak of white -
a stranger, drenched inside a wash of lights.

Light wraps me in a coat of fear,
Holding me unsure, as if in darkness.

~~~~

Superheroes

Superman is a fraud, just like me.
All we have is what the cosmos gives us.
We deal with our bodies,
however strange they are -
The most we do is cry about it.
In dark rooms, I search in vain for reasons to whine.
I'm no different from the spacey goons and supermen
that walk through time.
Still, some look at me, seeing strength.
They see these weaknesses
and think I must be somehow stronger than I look.
"I Guess." I blink.
Each compliment a shaky boulder,
placed upon my bony shoulders.

~~~~

They say that poets and rock stars must end with glorious steam
and burned fuel,
with a furious halt, like a drunken freight train.
Such will not be my undoing.
I move on slowly, and I diffuse slowly.

I wake. A day goes. I sleep. I wake.

Each cycle is a small undoing, each day a choice, each choice a
disconnection.
Simply, I will disappear one day. (for I have often wished to do so)
as a wisp of smoke diffused from a powder puff.

~~~~

Cancer's Proposal

I'll be your little lobster, if you'd like,
and oh, what a wondrous lover I could be!

I know of men who say they know
true love, but there is a sea that knows
constructed love is not love;
unchanging cannot be undying;
the ocean pulls and tugs at walls
that once seemed so strong.

I am of that ocean,
and though my body stands
a mile short of man's,
I've felt those earthly waters,
comfortable as sorrow, filled with joy;
they touch the skin
like pillows, moist
with tears and morning dew.

That sea is within us,
yet we did not create it
and it is not for our control.
Be passive. The waves will come
and lick our skin
until it finally draws us in.

Why do you falter
at my offering of passion?
True, I am the thing you see;
strange lobster boy with ragged claws,
clumsy crustacean beast
that adores you.
I remain,
honorably and proudly, subhuman.
I do not speak the word I do not understand.
I am content to feel its power
and let its currents guide me.

I am I. I've nothing more
or less to be
but this body (strange
as it is beautiful, beautiful
as it is amusing):
a reddened face,
a shell,
two twisted claws,
and two obsidian eyes,
eyes that yearn and deeply care,
that can embrace,
that need you,

eyes that see you
as a radiant mermaid.

Let us, my lady be wed by the sea!

~~~~

Stephanie's Poem

I wear a silver locket
with a balled up poem inside
that pushes
the little door
half open, almost breaks
the teeny clasp.
(My boyfriend gave it to me.)
I keep it by my heart
reminding me that
the nicest things
we keep inside
our hearts
don't always
fit exactly.

Freedom

You sit upon the high mountain,
And look at the vast land below you.
You spread your powerful wings,
Your soft feathers, of sheer silk,
Your mighty claws, of sheer stone.

As you glide into the crystal blue sky,
You glide into another world.
A world where nothing is confined,
A world where everything is free
From the bonds of the earth.

Lord, let me fly with the mighty eagle,
The master of the sky.
Take me on a pilgrimage
To the eagle ...
To the sky.

~~~~

Sweet Sounds

The sound, so calm,
It enters my ears.
The sound of the butterfly
As it flutters in the
soft, balmy air.
It is high,
Then low,
Then it is gone forever.
It is only left in my memories.

The sound, so harsh,
It enters my ears.
The sound of the storm,
As it slowly consumes

Everything in its path.
It is north,
Then south,
Then it is gone forever.
It is only left in my memories.

~~~

In dreams, I move into the past,
letting time roll out of my stoney eyes.
Each careful step forgets the last.

Stiff air of morning, too cold to relax;
I rarely know a reason to rise.
In dreams, I move into the past.

Energy is rare and hard to grasp.
I walk from fire to deadened fires.
Each careful step forgets the last.

Evenings of verse, longwinded and fast
(my verse is prose and dreamy cries).
In dreams, I move into the past.

I speak to those whose voices pass;
I'm silent when among the wise.
Each careful step forgets the last.

Though, evening's air is pure and vast,
And though I've learned to disregard the lies,
In slowing dreams, I move into the past
And pray each step forgets the last.

Zen and the Art of Socializing

I quickly fell for her: the girl who sat across from me – no book or
phone or notes to read were in her precious space. Her bench was
nearly twenty feet away. My thought was like a beating heart – it
never stopped or turned or swayed it's slow, recurring drive: "Go
speak, go speak, go speak," it cried. The tension lingered in the air
and pulled around my form. And she, with startling grace betrayed
my wants. She lit a cigarette.

~~~~

the nerves
turn still –

air cuts across them
like ice
reminding me
to forget how to feel

~~~~

The clouds form
brilliant, flaming figure skaters
and purple shrouded nomads,
contemplating sleep.

I sit with you
and wonder
if the sky would ever break
like ice.

Now, night arrives.
Colors expire:
slowly the world goes grey
and then a darker grey –
a dignified, stoic grey
before the black.

~~~

In bed, after they had drained each other,
he quivered, not knowing
who to be at that moment.
He whispered the words again
and waited, troubled yet unshocked by the long silence

broken
the moment she pulled him along
side of herself telling him
goodnight.
She left while he was still naked,
He cried
soft tears of relief
at the loneliness
wrapping around him
in her absence.

~~~~

New World, July 21, 1969
On the other side of the moon
we find the first swallow.
His feathers
grow brittle in the cold.
His eyes blink through the darkness.
He followed us here
and got lost
in divine delusions
that comforted us,
somehow.

~~~~

Once I saw shining in myself a picture-dreamer.
I saw for me a
slender,
fragile
delicate,
beautiful body form,
a crafted version of my true defective shell.
Simply dressed,
a rogue in cape and silver cane.
My every word and action,
a poem,
a command to live and dream.

~~~~

Contact Lens
my body, still
you held me
in your gaze
"look up"
and so my eyes lifted
my breath paused
knowing no other closeness
my eyes and yours: contact
my eyes and your finger: contact
"blink"
and then:
focus

~~~~

Dead branches
frame iced windows of
blue-white glass.

~~~~

About feelings close to one's heart:
True words drop
     Hard

         cold

            dry

               dead,
smothered by confused screams.

~~~~

"I love you."

     A word, a knife
     with darkness on its mirrored edge.
     such peace I bleed.

~~~~

Sentiments off walls
of empty halls do bounce
and echo loudly.

~~~~

Aftermath of a soulful conversation:

     Now my dear,
     This snake between us
     May coil us together,

     or send us screaming
     In opposing directions.

~~~~

morning:
into daydream I rise again

my careful steps
each to forget the last

She flies,

a silent,
playful bird,

in and out
of dreams

and life.

~~~~

Peace on Earth

arrives
as silent missiles
arc across the orange sky,
landing, with
subtle, silent,
explosions

In the Looking Glass

are pinprick
reflections
of
all the faces
in my life.

~~~~

Mature Lust

The soul soaks in beautiful pain
to press against a body strange

not to feel the flesh
in sweaty -- cold embraces

but -- to drift, fall down

through softer -- deeper spaces.

~~~~

She had eyes like money;
      inscrutable eyes that folded around me,
      holding my mind with fire arms.
(the cheap grace of arms and explosives
      flashed in me with lusty fires and)
I cursed the high balcony that separated me
      from this drugstore bride,
      her cheekbone blessed with a lavender bruise.
But stillness lingered in me, and I knew no lust or sympathy
would sway me from my height.
My horses would never drive her chariot to Paris.

~~~~

If I were Salvador Dali, I'd paint you as a deep red sunset with blue eyes. I'd paint you reflected in a pond, your image shivering in the breeze. You're far away now, and hard to imagine. When we were children, we played games together. Later, you wanted to play house - you wanted a husband, but I never really got that game. I'd rather something wild - on a highway together with Springsteen on the radio, headed for the mountains. Is freedom not what you desire? Or do you still play house? Remember our childhood - we were mirrors. If you could lay next to me and watch my gaze, you'd see yourself as you really are. Inside, you too are a wild soul. I desire a love that could kill us both. Love is a knife. Darkness is its edge. The crocuses bloom between us, and we can choose to live explosively before we die.

~~~~

I watch you read,
the lines on your face
echoing the lines of the poem.
Both are emotional maps.
I'm not a skilled cartographer
and your map is difficult
For me to understand.

I wonder how many pieces of me you find.
I wonder if I want you to find them -
I took such care to hide them indiscreetly. They're like little dolls,
dressed in costumes and buried
under distracting piles of charms
and toys. The doll's face never changes.

It is always me.
When you find them,
we'll pretend together
that they don't exist.
There will be a special tension
in the air between us.
That is what we share.

Do you know I wrote this poem for you
and for that moment?

In the meantime, we both
trace lines of silent words,
leading to tea cups, raindrops,
moonlit walks, candles,
conversations, and deep connections
that almost exist between us.

~~~~

Many years have we
traveled across the
vast desert in
search of our great
leader and we have
found him not upon
the earthly plane, but
in the hearts of
man – and under
his leadership we shall rise
above all and destroy the
fowl creatures that
call themselves humans.

Apocalypse is not
the work of God – nor
is it the work of
Satan. It is merely
the product of our
own stupidity.

~~~~

All things that are
lost may be found,

All things that are asleep
may be wakened.

Turn the key in the lock
open your mind

As the scales fall from your
eyes,
you will see new visions you never
perceived before.

~~~~

The cemetery earth is cool; the brown grass, the aging flowers are
dry reminders of life's short span;
the stones ponder life in silence and regret, crumbling
into faces of old men gazing into chessboards;
the trees are twisted and gnarled,
dry corpses of mangled animals;
the blue-black sky hangs here, still and dim and silent;
pale stars watch over us with apathetic eyes;
our friends lie around us, scattered like soldiers
dead or wounded or starry eyed and stoned.

Whatever warmth is here is my own.

~~~~

Meditation on a Foggy Night

Lying in the grass,
I'm gazing up into a bowl of smoky glass
with a white cherry floating at it's center.
My breath is slow. Ghosts crawl
from my mouth when I exhale.
I am wrapped in cool air and wet grass.

My legs tingle; the electric earth beneath them
slides it's hands through me,
wraps its arms around the inside of me.
A single drop of rain rolls off a branch, kissing my forehead
and I remember suddenly who my mother is.
Home is where you come from.
It is where you lie.
Tonight I rest in both places.

Revelations to a Stupid Kid

I. I rarely considered
how many roses
were left
for me

by friends or lovers
whose names
I never learned.

II. I let Doubt become a friend;
I let Doubt hold me
when I stepped back
from concrete consolation.

Doubt is the blade
that cut me from reality.

III. The most powerful microscope
is hardest to control;

when focused deeply
for the small shreds

it's easy
to slip past

signs directed
at the naked eye.

IV. Unconditional love is
mostly
a game.

V. The deepest emotion is lavender
wrapped in blood.

VI. If I find myself
wrapped in some one

I might not know who to be.

Is it really searching
That makes me who I am?

The Death of an Angel

The pale, yellowish
flesh hangs loosely on
his expressionless face.

His eyes, once crystalline
With the knowledge and
the understanding of
Humanity

Are now only
Blue white marbles
Staring at his immediate
Future a great distance behind him.

It pains me to realize the
hatred the world loved
him with. He was the
puzzle piece which
didn't quite fit; He was
an angel in this hell that
you built; He cared for
everyone who never
cared for him; He was
the last meaningful thing
in your world of unmeaning.

He looked at me, and uttered the last significant words ever uttered.

"What good is life, when life is lived for death?
 What good is caring, when care is not returned?

Once I tried to save the world;
The world has committed suicide.

The death of humanity marks
the death of an angel."

More Tributes

RJ was such a special part of mine, my sister's and our family's lives. There are so many small memories; his yellow brace, swimming, tolerating his dad's jokes, the way he held his breath when he was laughing so hard at something, that are forever woven into the fabric of our lives.

I feel so lucky to have known him. He had such a wise way about him, even my earliest memories when he was a toddler he seemed like a wise old man. I remember his sweet smile, his eyelashes and eyes. He contributed so much in such little time. I was blown away when I read his poetry. The depth of feeling it evoked was on a level of someone who had traveled the world and was many years older. He is someone so special that I will never forget and I am blessed to have known him. Every time I say my youngest daughter's middle name, I am reminded of him and thankful to have been a part of his world for a time.

Alicia Heller

So many memories ... where do I start? A new baby in the family! Fighting with my sister over who gets to hold that new baby R.J., even though both of us were probably way too young to be even holding a baby! Competing for his attention. Spending time with him was pure joy. He made me laugh, smile and fall in love with his adorableness. His yellow brace ... and that crazy table that wrapped around the yellow brace, where we played for hours on end with him. I remember so much about R.J. His adorable eyes. He smiled with those eyes. His laugh! We would laugh at his laugh. It was funny even to hear it. There was very little noise that would come out, yet he was laughing so hard, we knew he was bursting out and we were too.
Growing older together.
Sleeping over at Uncle Randy and Aunt Holly's house. Walking with RJ in his stroller, down the street to the edge of the Mullica River. Aunt Holly let me push the stroller all by myself - so proud to do that. Then in Absecon. I loved sleeping over and spending time with all of the Corradinos. We were even allowed to babysit RJ at times!

Sparky- lovable dog, but wouldn't listen for $H!T. RJ would simply roll his eyes and we would all laugh.

Florida trips in West Palm Beach and multiple families smashing into the purple Nova all at one time, no seatbelts of course. We were safe. No worries, Eddie was driving. Uncle Sal and Uncle Randy slathered in baby oil with iodine. Sun rays were way safer back then. Eating, eating and more eating. Family time.

Growing older together.

RJ singing Journey's - Don't Stop Believin'. I was older and didn't even know what he was singing. He always knew the latest pop culture.

Jokes, laughter, patience. I remember a lot of patience. Calm, he always seemed so calm. Thought out. Reflective. Mature.

Ridge - RJ's right hand buddy.

Poems, lots of them. "On an Outing with My Son," "A Moment Dropped," "Sunshower Song," and my favorite - "The Window."

I'm now also remembering as we got older how we would send emails back and forth to say our hellos.

"Heya Lex ... so, so ~so~ sorry I haven't been in touch. School got really busy, and then my wheelchair broke and I couldn't use the computer ... "

... yet his forever optimistic outlook on everything as shown in his very next sentence ...

" .. But overall I am doing pretty well."

Always a positive attitude no matter what he was dealing with at the time.

RJ's beautiful crush on Belinda- "Bel". His ability to share his vulnerable-ness in his words ..

"The only things I really know are my loneliness, and the fact that talking with Bel makes me feel good. I have to confess that I am not the world's greatest hugger. My arms are weak, and I need help getting them around a person's shoulders. Sadly, Bel didn't know to do this, so I improvised as best I could. I smiled and leaned my head down to give her some extra check/shoulder contact."

I marveled at how beautifully expressive RJ was.

Most importantly I remember (and miss) RJ's sense of humor, yet that memory actually makes me smile each and every time I think about him.

Thank you for sharing RJ with me. He will never disappear from my memory.

Alexis Rewick

The Window
I have spent
Many long tedious hours
Weaving, as I sit
Staring out the window
Like a man in prison,
Waiting to be released.
I have formed a new Universe, and placed it
On the other side of the
Window
It is in this world
Where my destiny lies.

It was beautiful on the other side!
It was the same,
Yet it was different.
It was more amazing,
More, glorious.

("An excerpt from The Window by RJ Corradino")

Dear R.J.,

Each stage of life is filled with different people and experiences that vary in significance. My early years are filled with memories of hanging out and growing-up alongside you. My sisters and I love you so much. You were only two years younger, but FINALLY, I got to play big sister to someone! Truth is, we were really more like equals ... okay, fine, you were more mature. Always sharing an insightful, wise-beyond-your-years understanding of the world. I only knew how amazing I felt being around you and your parents, and I always wanted to see you guys more. I hated that you lived too far away for more frequent visits. Life got busier and things changed, but the plan was always to come back around to each other. I miss you so very much and wish you were here. I would love to see your smile, to hug you, to hear your voice, to sit and talk. I hope you now run wild and free with sunshine on your face. Thank you for sharing a piece of yourself and for perfect memories that I can call on anytime. You are so very loved and cherished.

Love Always and forever, Althea
Althea David

For sure, RJ is not truly gone, nor will he ever be. His impact on so many of us in the short span of time we had him was monumental. Many live decades and pass from this life without ever leaving a footprint. Not so RJ! His wit, his humor, his brilliance with words touched so many. He lives on in our family as we recount wonderful visits, vacations, parties, swimming, laughing; seeing his beautiful smiling face with that perpetual twinkle in his eyes. There are so many "RJ" stories we share and it brings joy to our hearts. Our family has grown immensely in these last 20 years and every one of our new additions knows RJ.

No he will never be truly gone, for he lives on in our hearts forever.

Ruth Lazzara

One of the crazy memories is the time we all drove to the state park in Maryland in the van and we were stopped by the park police. And it turned into another happy RJ memory. Unforgettable.

Ed Lazzara

Dear Holly and Randy,

Please see how much RJ has touched and inspired me:

How can 20 years have passed. It seems like yesterday. I will always remember his infectious smile. Oh, those magic tricks he would make me fall for. And he couldn't wait to reveal some new gadget in his state-of-the-art bedroom (which usually was beyond my comprehension, and he knew that too). Zipping around the pool was always a highlight. And when the cousins came, that was a ready-made party with a ton of laughter. RJ always seemed like a big brother to our kids, and never missed an opportunity to pull a prank. Then when it was time to settle down, we'd get blankets and pillows and cuddle on the floor watching TV, with Gregory and Danielle snuggled next to him and Sparky right there. I can feel the warmth just thinking about it. There was the time that RJ went to the Rolling Stones concert and the guys got to go right up front with him. Wow, that smile on RJ's face afterwards spoke more than words. A more serious time was when he would speak to me quietly and just said to take care of her, she is going to be okay. RJ shared all his compassion and love at such a young age, and yet he was so wise. Honestly, I never met someone so loving, caring, funny, quirky and compassionate as RJ. He has remained in my heart in a very special place. Thank you, Holly and Randy for sharing RJ with me, and us. He was truly a gift.

Love, Brenda
Brenda Martello

One could only be inspired by the courage and fortitude RJ demonstrated as a child, as a teen and as a young man. His sense of humor and wit entertained us and always brought a smile to our faces. His accomplishments were truly special. We thank Holly and Randy for giving RJ a voice by way of his writings so we can remain in touch with his spirit always.

John Martello

I feel so lucky to have been friends with RJ growing up. He was the coolest person I knew. We shared a love of good music.
Whether it was something new that he introduced me to like Nirvana Unplugged or putting on a classic record like Let It Be, I knew every time we hung out we would be listening to something cool and authentic. Which is exactly how I would choose to describe my friend RJ-cool and authentic. I miss him and look back fondly at the times we had. Great memories.

Greg Martello

When I think of RJ many things come to mind immediately. First being the calendar photo of RJ dressed as a clown with a bright yellow wig, and when I would walk by and ask my mom, who is this? she would happily say, "That's RJ!" I remember smiling right back at him, as if he was right there in the room with us. I also think about his love of music, rock and roll, and of course poetry and writing. He was one of my main influencers for my own poetry and we were kindred spirits in that way. My fondest memories are when we had the New Year's Eve parties. We would watch Randy flip the pizza crusts as RJ made jokes and laughed with us at the table. He was truly a part of our family and he is so dearly missed. When I sat down to write this at first, I honestly didn't even know where to start, and now I think I know why. RJ cannot be remembered by just words on paper (even though that definitely helps), but RJ was a spirit, a force, an energy that is greater than just these little words. RJ lived so much more than his brief life with us, and his soul was wiser than anyone I have ever met. He lives on through each of us, and we should strive to meet each day more like RJ, with humility, humor and tremendous bravery.

Danielle Martello

As only having been around RJ in my early childhood years, I don't have too many detailed memories. However, what I can remember fondly is always being super excited as a young boy going to visit RJ and the whole family. Those were weekends I will never forget. In a way I still feel like I got to know RJ through the stories I've been told by my family that got to know RJ very well. Stories of rock and roll, a larger than life smile, and a constant joy to be around. I will forever remember and cherish my days with RJ.

Love,
Dylan
Dylan Martello

Dear RJ,

Ginny and I wish we had known you from the time you were born so that we would have experienced your love, joy and talents that we so often talk about with your mom and dad.

In many ways, we feel we have known you since you were born through the love and relationship we have with your parents and extended family.

Your mom and dad are our best friends and they carry your love with them every day and it transcends to us. We share funny stories and some serious moments as well as your very talented poetry.

Although we never met you in person, we know we have met you spiritually and your memory will live on with us through the friendship we have with your mom and dad.

You are deeply missed but never forgotten and always in our thoughts and prayers.

Rest in peace, RJ we love you.

Frank Valente

RJ Corradino

A great love of life.
A kind and joyful spirit.
Wise beyond his years.
And a whole lot of fun to be with!

These are some of the words that come to mind when I think of RJ. There are many more. He was smart, creative, kind, and very funny; extremely polite and always cooperative. He rarely complained though I know there were times he was in pain. He was patient with everyone, except himself. Oh, was he hard on himself. RJ was courageous; he persevered through things I'm not so sure I could. He definitely faced more obstacles and difficulties than most; yet you wouldn't have known. Allow me to share one example, in hopes of creating pictures from words.

RJ used a power wheelchair, at high speed, all the time; fortunately he was an excellent driver. Despite excellent care, like all mechanical things, occasionally it needed repairs. Simple repairs could be done at home, but now and then, the chair had to be taken. Most vendors provided a loaner. Unfortunately, loaner power chairs were rarely available. So for a few days, often more, RJ had to use a manual chair in which, despite our best efforts, he was often poorly positioned. Good positioning was the key to his function but more importantly to his comfort. So there he was: unable to drive or move himself, limited in daily tasks; often unable to access his computer, which he loved and which served as a gateway to and sanctuary from the world. Often he was uncomfortable or in pain, yet except maybe for Mom and Dad, no one would ever know.

He taught me so much about so many things. Yes, I learned about wheelchairs and posture and adaptive equipment; but there was so much more. He allowed me try new techniques on him. If he knew I went to a continuing ed. course, he would greet me at his next session with, "so what new technique are we trying today." He became my 'go-to' for treatment ideas with younger children. He was so good at coming up with ways to make it more fun, that I also consulted him about things to do with teenagers I worked with in youth ministry.

He came up with my department's Halloween costume every year. When there were only 4 of us in the PT department we were the four seasons and when we were bigger we were a box of crayons. We were always the hit of the Halloween parade. Often I reflect on how observant and how truly selfless he was. You see the games and activities he suggested were always enjoyed by all and yet I doubt that he was ever able to participate in any of them.

I remember being concerned about how he was accepting all of this when he was a tween or teen. I gingerly managed to bring it up one day. I asked if being in a wheelchair bothered him. I'll never forget his answer. He took a bit of time, then answered yes and no. Yes of course he wished he could do things that other people who walk do, but "I've come to enjoy being a spectator and we get great parking."

RJ was an avid reader. His favorites at that time were Hitchhiker's Guide to the Galaxy and everything by Tolkien. We discussed evolution, music, politics and movies. He was a techno-wizard; more than once he taught me things on the computer I would have never known or understood without his help. Most days he was the teacher and I was the student.

RJ had a tremendous impact on my life and still does. If I'm faced with a challenge, or watch The Lord of the Rings, and most assuredly on every Halloween, I close my eyes and he is there. He made me a better therapist, youth minister, and person. More than all of these, I had the honor and privilege of knowing him as a friend; for this I am forever grateful.

Pat Bentley

There are people that you meet in life who become a part of your spirit without you even realizing it. Dear RJ was one of those people for me. I can vividly remember meeting RJ for the first time when he was around 4 years old when his father, Randy, brought him into the Prudential Office for a visit. My first impression was there was such a brightness around this little fella with the big beautiful smile. He was so relaxed and friendly with people even at that age, such maturity. All of that was felt, but the thing that stayed with me even to this day is when he spoke, his voice was like a bell. It is hard to explain but it was like music, clear and pure. I have never mentioned that before, but I have always to this day remembered his voice. I look back and I wonder why this made such an impression on me, for I have never again experienced this from anyone else but I can replay in my head, hearing that little 4 year old boy speaking in that pure clear voice that reminded me of a little beautiful bell.

I was with the family at RJ's passing and the strength that I saw especially from his parents and other family members is woven into my spirit and has helped me through my life's journey. I was so proud to be asked to sing at RJ's funeral. It gave me the opportunity to thank RJ for the lessons I learned from knowing him and knowing about him. Such an Amazing Grace.

Cheryl Bythewood Mapp
Testimonial for RJ's book

I'm sad to say that I only met RJ once. He was six or seven years old and we met at the one and only Corradino family reunion that cousin Mike and RJ's grandfather, Uncle Tutti, put together in 1988. RJ was a happy, joyful child. He was in a wheelchair and all the children played with him. I can still picture him in my mind's eye that day. A beautiful smile.

Fran and I had moved to Virginia for the Air Force in 1966 and we never moved back to New Jersey. And so often as you get older and have a family, home and career, you don't have enough time to go visit relatives.

Fortunately for me, RJ's father, Randy and I became good friends and he shared family home movies of RJ with me so I feel I know RJ as a child. Randy also shared RJ's poetry with me. Needless to say, it blew me away.

What I found so fascinating was that for someone so young he has distilled the universal into the individual. His reactions to life are of a much older person. By that I mean the thought provoking imagery. The word play! It is clear that he was a sensitive soul. An "old soul," well beyond his years.

And at times I sense an Asian poetic form, existentialism in his writing, and at one point Buddhism. I am a great fan of both existential and Buddhist philosophy and psychology so this really resonates with me. And believe it or not the two are closely related because they deal with the essentials of life, the finality of life, and the suffering we face in life.

Especially in ancient Chinese poems like Li Po, the Chinese poet. This really comes out in RJ's poem "This is stillness." He could've been writing 2000 years ago in China or Korea or Vietnam. And this poem is the work of a very accomplished poet.

And in "Untitled," he writes, "I wake. A day goes. I sleep. I wake." This poem seems to me to embody the three things that I love so much. Asian poetry, existentialism and Buddhism. And then in the last stanza he talks about choice. As a person and as a psychologist, choice is at the heart of everything I'm about. I believe so much in the power of "choice." Our lives are made up of billions of choices. And there's an Italian existentialist writer Nicolo Abbagbano, who's book "Positive Existentialism" focuses on this. We have the power to change our lives every minute by the choices we make.

In "About a broken compass" he talked about "chosen direction" but the imagery about a compass is more so about our lives and where we're going, or not going. Amazing!

And the "piece de resistance," his poem, "Cancer's Proposal" amazed and inspired me. He writes: "I am of that ocean, and though my body stands a mile short of man's, (I think that of my body, superman I'm not, bookworm I am!) I felt those earthly waters, comfortable as sorrow, filled with joy, they touch the skin like pillows, moist with tears and morning dew." Amazing! Profound!

The next stanza, "that sea is within us, yet we do not create it and it is not for our control." So powerful, so beautiful! Again I sense existentialism and Buddhism. His poetry expresses his courage. Conversely his courage is reflected in his poetry. He goes on, "I remain, honorably and proudly, subhuman. I do not speak the word I do not understand. I am content to feel it's power and let it's current guide me."

My favorite line, "I am I. I've nothing more or less to be but this body" kinda reminds me of the Frank Sinatra song "My Way" (where he sings "what is a man, what has he got, if not himself then he has naught) there's more to that song stanza. You might want to look it up because some of the other lines speak to RJ's life.

And then I'm almost speechless, with his poem "On an outing with my son!" The power of that poem. The longing expressed in that poem! The wisdom in the stanza "I thought of my youth: such faith I had in destiny, God's loving plan of endless earthly lessons. I knew or used to know that overcoming a true burden meant first resigning to it." Again reflections of Buddhism. A wisdom beyond his years!

And in "Untitled" where he writes, "when we speak, I want my words to gently fall against your heart, letting slip the latches to your mind." Isn't this what all of us want when we talk to someone, especially a loved one or a lover? And what a lover he might have made, or maybe was, because the English grammar book I purchased was dedicated to him by the author, who said "she never had a more loving friend."

And then I think my favorite, well so many poems/lines, especially were favorites, (Ha) is: "Super Heroes" where he starts out, "Superman is a fraud, just like me." How often do we, well let me speak for myself, I feel like a fraud? But then he goes on with something that is profound: "All we have is what the cosmos gives us." Can you imagine this coming from someone who is a teenager or only 20 years old!

"We deal with our bodies, however strange they are -- the most we do is cry about it. In dark rooms, I search in vain for reasons to whine. I am no different from the Spacey goons and supermen that walk through time!" I can imagine he might have cried about the unfairness of life, vis-à-vis, his illness and life in a wheelchair. I know when in the darkness I have lamented much, and my life has been a cakewalk compared to his.

Life is so inexplicable, so unfair, so strange, so perverse in many ways. And if RJ had a normal length lifespan to live, might he have become a poet laureate! Or was his short life, and his illness, formative so that he distills a lifetime into 20 years. I write this with tears, but with no answers. Only anger at the unfairness of it all.

So when you think about it RJ distilled a lifetime of all of that into 20 years, which breaks my heart to say it. But on the other hand, and I never use this word, I stand in awe, or as the young people say "awesome!"

Randy told me that in RJ's last year of college, he attended a Christmas party at his professor's house. When he came home he was so proud to tell his father that when the professor introduced the other students he would say, "this is my student." But when he introduced RJ he said, "I would like you to meet a poet." It meant so much to him.

Richard Stockton College lost a poet. The Corradino family lost a poet. We all lost a voice in the great Italian/Sicilian/American tradition of poetry. His poetry speaks for itself, it speaks for him and his poetry speaks to all of us.

Mary Jane Oliver (September 10, 1935-January 17, 2019) was an American poet who won the National Book Award and the Pulitzer Prize. She said: "The poet is speaking to the person who will read this poem 50 years after I'm dead." That is why this book of his poetry is so important.

RJ died much too young - before he had a chance to fulfill his destiny. But for those of us left behind there is an old African proverb that might give us some comfort: "Where love exists, night never falls." Because those we love will always be in our hearts. And night will never fall on our love for RJ and for his poetry!

Gandolfo Corradino

For RJ

Sitting in my old blue truck
that's got so much rust under its belt
I'm surprised the body holds to the frame,
I think back to the day
we laid you here
then left to our homes to eat sweets and forget.

One year since and I've been unable to do that.
It was raining then and the wind
could not stop itself
from moving.
There were so many faces I had never seen,
offering me good solitude.
I wanted to drink that day into pleasantries,
drink till I passed out
and woke to myself,
to what I believed and questioned.
All the poems I read on death
had not prepared me.
And tonight, nothing can stop the wind;
it is again moving
over your grave
where grass has yet to grow.
To that I think it was not your time
or the earth does not want you.
I know there is meaning in the way I grieve,
staring through my pitted windshield
down at dirt,
dirt that scatters like shards of stone
and the carved names they own.
Perhaps I should scratch deep into the soil
open old wounds
to get to the casket,
then crack the glue at the side seam.
Hear you tell me it was just a joke
and we can be done with this foolishness.
But these things can never happen
instead this rain will break me into so many parts
there will not be enough hands to count
the amount of discord
scattered across this field.
From this truck I want to read
you lines from poems I will write
before I ever think the image through.
Before I even know what I would write
before I begin to tear at myself
and fall onto pages.

I'm afraid to start the engine.
Afraid to turn the key
that turns my life
that is newly orphaned
yet still sensing some magnificence in it all.

Michael Jemal

Dear Randy and Holly,

Nancy and I remember meeting RJ for the first time at the Kessler
Memorial Hospital in Hammonton, NJ when he was born in 1979.
We have many fond memories from the times we would get
together with you two and RJ and our two boys Michael and Mark.
Nancy reminded me of the time we told Mark when he was two
and RJ was a baby that he had to give his bottle to RJ because he
was a new baby and he needed it more than Mark. We were trying
to break Mark of the bottle. I especially remember RJ, Randy, John
Martello and myself going to the movies on a Saturday afternoon at
the Tilton theater to see the Jerkey Boys new movie. We had to
sneak out so no one would recognize us. Nancy had a surprise
birthday party for me on my 50th and of course Randy and John
had to remind me what I looked like wearing glasses with my
slightly larger nose by wearing nose glasses which I believe RJ
really got a kick out of as he gave me a birthday present that I still
have today. It was a CD the Best of the Blues Brothers.

RJ will forever be in Our Thoughts and in Our Hearts. He was a
Kind, Caring, Talented young man and a good friend like you two.

Chuck and Nancy Leeds

I remember RJ being a sweet little boy being with him in your
swimming pool in your Absecon house. Such a wonderful little boy
with such a sweet personality. You and Holly were such wonderful
parents who gave him all your love.

John Blanos

Essays and More

My Caffeinated Memoirs

Some months ago, I awoke with a terrible headache and stiff neck. Knowing that stimulants could cause such ailments; it seemed a wise idea to skip my normal caffeine rituals that day. I had already gone a weekend without a fix, just by accident. I could go another day. For several hours, I competed with pain in my head, neck, and shoulders, along with a growing craving for a certain caramel-colored, carbonated beverage.

I survived until 5:30 that evening, when my headache started to get worse. It seemed it wasn't a 'hopped up' headache, so I decided there was no harm in giving in to my urge. It sounds like a very thoughtful decision when I word it that way. A better way of saying it: I caved. I took a can of Coca Cola Classic, and admired it's shimmering red, metallic finish for a moment. I cracked it's top and stole a sip - which soon became a series of greedy, slurping gulps. My headache dissolved in minutes. That was a red flag for me. That made me wonder if I was enjoying this for more than the taste. It seemed I got a headache from abstaining from it – that sounded like a dependency. That worried me, and I decided to try giving up caffeine.

It seems a bit silly in retrospect. Caffeine never dominated my life – It was always just a habit. In the mornings, I'd always sip some herbal, caffeinated tea while I listened to some soothing music – Led Zeppelin II or Fresh Cream. What was more important to me, was the Coke I'd drink after lunch while I watched reruns of MASH.

Let me tell you a bit about my taste in Coke - I'm very particular about all this. I drink from the can with a straw. Doing otherwise will subtly change the amount of fizz, and this is intolerable. Pouring a Coke over ice is completely unethical. It becomes watered down – the natural balance that perfects this special drink is destroyed. There is no turning back. I don't care if your ice is crushed, cubed, or ring shaped – the moment your Coke makes contact, it's flavor will be demolished. I despise vending machines – the ones that drop the paper cup and fill it with a beverage and ice. These go against every Coke principal that I hold dear. The soda in these contraptions has never touched a can, and the infamous no-ice button never works (or if it does work, you're given 1/3 of the glass). Making things worse, these machines disrupt the delicate Coca Cola balance by mishandling the syrup/fizz/water ratios. I've yet to see one of these come close to making a good drink – any drink, let alone a delicate flavored masterpiece like Coke.

You see, Coca Cola is nothing if not a balance. The carbonation is a natural ally to the cool temperature of a refrigerated can. The soothing, metallic bitterness of the caffeine sits juxtaposed to the almost sickening sweet syrup. If you leave a can unattended – which I often do – some mystic changes unfold. The soda warms in perfect harmony with a loss of fizz. As this happens, the subtle flavors come forward. It almost seems like a metaphor for life – although I can't fathom what it may mean. At any rate, it tastes surprisingly wonderful.

This is what I'd do with the can I opened after lunch. I'd drink almost half of it, and then let it stand for a few hours. I'd sip at it, but only periodically. It was always fun to note the subtle taste changes as it grew warm and flat. At 1:00, I'd sit down to do my writing. I'd nurse whatever remained of that same can – usually a fair amount – and let my caffeine infused blood stimulate my creativity. So, I see now that my habit was not very strong – only a can and some tea each day. Half the time, the tea wasn't even caffeinated. Still, I felt moved to give it up. Tea was easy to drop. I found decaf tea tasted better to me. It lacked the unpleasant rusty metal flavor that caffeine carries. Coca Cola was hard to replace – it seemed to rely on that bitter taste, it was part of the balance. I tried caffeine free Coke. My theory was correct – this was much too sweet. After stumbling back into my Coke habit three times, I tried quitting again with ginger ale as a pinch hitter for Coke. This was the longest I lasted – almost two months without a single sip of Coke. At that time, my desires were getting out of hand. I needed a fix. I didn't care if it was caffeinated. I just needed a Coke. I needed a caramel colored, carbonated beverage in a red can. I had a revelation; Dr. Pepper. It had the flavor I needed – I knew it did. And I didn't think it had caffeine. I bought a case. My spirit collapsed when I read the ingredients: water, sugar, sugar, more sugar, caramel coloring, caffeine.

I did some soul searching that day. I realized how little soda I really drank – compared to some people. I realized that all that time I had been eating chocolate without even blinking. I never did give up caffeine. I also discovered that caffeine was a natural pain killer – which was why it defeated my headache. It had nothing to do with 'dependency.'

After a little thought, I was happy to rebegin indulging my addiction. All great writers need vices, don't they? At least mine is legal. I cracked the can and drank of it. Dr. Pepper is still making me a new and better man.

In my seventeen odd years of existence on this planet, I have been guilty of a horrid, even grotesque crime. I read. I read a lot. I read so much that my eyes have been getting angry with me lately for making them squint and focus on tiny print squished into volumes of thin flimsy strips of parchment. Despite the fact that I'll most likely be legally blind by the time I graduate, there is good news.

My love of reading places me among the elite. You see, in my generation, an infatuation with words is a scarcity, even to the point of being disturbing. The problem with our nation's youth lies within the educational system. Think about it. By the time we enter 5th grade, we've grown to hate everything having any connection with school. That includes the bloodthirsty English teacher who failed you on the <u>Johnny Tremain</u> test (Abseconites will appreciate this). Sooner or later, all other books become guilty of boredom by association. As a result, many teens end up ignoring the context of a book, and instead hang around movie theaters in search of the latest Jackie Chan movie (now there's culture at its finest) or the next episode of *Baywatch* (or Babewatch, which ever name you prefer). I think everyone should realize, however, that a good Steven King novel can be a lot more fun than Johnny Tremain (scratch that – I enjoyed good ol' Johnny the second time I read it; please forgive me, Abseconites).

I can feel the imminent question on your lips: "How do I tell a good book from a lousy one?" Hey, I can't do everything for you. Go to the bookstore! If you have a feeling that you don't belong there, pretend you're inside a Blockbuster Video, and it'll wear off eventually. Next, wander around, skimming over the covers of the books you pass by. Use the same tactics you use to pick out a movie, with one exception: don't get 28 books. I know when I pick out a movie, I like to get a bunch and watch them all weekend. DO NOT DO THIS, at least not on your first try. It takes lots of extended practice to consume more than a few hours of reading. Your brain might shut down after long exposure to culture.

So turn off the TV, for goodness sake, and get thee to a bookstore!

Generation Xmas

an experiment with clichés,
dedicated to Pamela Rice Hahn
(former poetry editor, www.blueroses.com)

God smiled down from heaven above,
and shined on us with all his love.
We felt new pennies from heaven
crashing on us; Towers of broken records
spoke to us our lives and dreams.
and then we talked about that, a little,
conjugating awesome.

The blind of earth, the huddled masses of America;
We are lost, we crowd in distant discount bookstores
in search of diets and religion. No one knows
the forest for the trees, but in these malls we miss
the forest altogether. Do we know the Gaps
for the slaps of consumerism?

There is a man looking a Spencer Gift horse in the mouth. If he
looked it in the ass, he might find the prize
(a remote control for his fart machine
or an x-rated slinky).

I pause, buying a hot dog.
Sinking my teeth into more pink flesh than I can chew, I feel I am
biting off my nose, and yet my face is not spited.
I smell my greasy lips, and wonder if my ears are jealous.
This hot dog tastes about as plain as the nose on my face.

How many curse words do these pictures say?
I'm almost done with my rant; will you respect me
when it's over? (No respect, no respect at all)
Otherwise, let us go then, you and I,
and fall into the Gap.
and then we'll sit,
contemplating Awesome.

The Day the Pleasure Factory Broke Down

Pallid whites, greys, spots of black danced (laughing) on the screen
like angry smoke.

Carlo's fat, furry hands
furiously beat the television set.
He let out a grunt,
and lifted the idol,
turning it around and exposing
the black, latex wiring
that once fed it life.
He tightened the cords,
working with the care
of a drunken surgeon
operating on his mother.

Continuing its mockery,
the television flickered the image
of a young man breaking his ass
on a wild bull,
and then the foul box went dead again. The grey smoke hissed
another laugh.

"Fuggin' cable."
There was a rodeo on ESPN2.
Poor Carlo would miss it.

Withdrawing,
he trembled and
put his frosted mug
of Coke and beer to his greasy lips,
wondering how he'd sleep the afternoon without the cold, flashing,
mad dreams made for him.

His children played outside,
blowing white mist from dandelions.

Blessed are the Meek ...

While it's been months since we've seen each other face to face, Belinda and I exchanged emails almost weekly for most of that time. Tonight, I had a class in the school's B wing, and I knew she had one in C. The two hallways were perhaps 20 feet from each other, and we both had class at 6:00PM. As much as I try to avoid using a high school word such as this one, I had a crush on her, and was looking for any chance to see her. This seemed a perfect time for a 'chance' meeting.

Like Peter Fonda in reverse, I strapped a leather watch to my wrist before I left. I rarely wear watches, but timing seemed important in this situation.

Arriving almost half an hour early, I wandered down the corridor and found a couple of guys to help me off the elevator. The two of them pushed the proper buttons and held the door, and then hitched a ride upstairs with me. I never ask folks to do that, but it's always nice when they offer. The cramped box we stood in did it's gentle shake, which frightened the two kind fellows. "I've seen worse," I chuckled. The doors opened, and making a right turn down the corridor, I left them. Now minor panic set in.

The C wing was almost directly in front of the elevator. I did the best I could to spin around to look for her without actually *appearing* to spin around and look. She wasn't there. I wanted to pull to the side, and wait for her, but that wasn't what happened. I don't know who was doing the steering, but I was moving toward class. I soon landed in my classroom and ended up chatting with the earlybirds about the film we watched last week.

I don't know if I planned to ask Bel out. I know I wanted to see her - I had no plans or even ideas outside of that.

I never dated in high school - I was simply uninterested. That may be a sign that I matured slowly, or just one that I had more common sense than my classmates. I didn't see any point in trying to date everything in sight, and I still don't. It seems more rational and romantic - rational romance is not an oxymoron – to wait, and allow time and human nature to draw me towards true love.

I wish I had some idea whether or not destiny is at work here. Right now, only half of me believes in that sort of thing –

maybe less than half. I wish I could think that true love awaits, and that we will be together for the rest of our lives. I've grown too cynical to think that way. I need to stick to tangible facts. I don't know what love is, or if it truly exists. Furthermore, I don't know Belinda well enough to even think about a future with her.

The only things I really know are my loneliness, and the fact that talking with Bel makes me feel good. In the spirit of living in the moment, this is all I need to know. All I can say is, I want to be closer to her. I can feel something unfolding - maybe it is friendship, or maybe it is more than that.

My class ended, and I drove - more slowly than normal - down the hallway. My eyes were darting about the scene in search of her. There was a group of chairs between the two wings, and I hoped to see her there, perhaps reading a book. She was not to be seen, and I worried that I had missed her.

I parked my chair to the side of the sitting area, angling my chair far enough toward the C wing door to see it without looking like I was staring at it. I checked my watch: 7:40. This class period didn't *technically* end until 8:00, so that was a good sign. In fact, she said that this class often ended late. I figured I would wait for her until ten after.

I sat there like a stalker, and tried to make my nervousness go away. The minor panic from before had returned, and it was gradually building up, like steam.

At five of, the C wing door opened. She didn't go through it, but I could see a herd of people waiting behind it. The students passed through the door one at a time as I watched.

I saw her.

She had a thin, blue windbreaker on, and her airy red hair was tucked through the back of a baseball cap. She smiled as she walked, her head turned away from me as she chatted with a friend.

I wondered what to do. My eyes went elsewhere, worrying that I'd look like I was waiting for her. I hoped she'd see me – it would be so much easier that way – but she continued without turning her head in my direction. A year, a month, a week, an hour ago I would have let my insecurities control me. I've let so many wonders walk pass me, and I feared Belinda would be one of them.

She had gone past me by now. "Hi Bel," I exclaimed, trying hard to sound surprised to see her. She turned, briskly saying goodbye to her friend, and greeting me with a hug.

Let me say a word or two about hugs. I think they're simply wonderful. There is no substitute for a good hug, and I believe that society desperately needs a few more good huggle-snugglers. Suffice to say, I was pleasantly surprised by her wonderful greeting. That said, I have to confess that I am not the world's greatest hugger. My arms are weak and I need help getting them around a person's shoulders. Sadly, Bel didn't know to do this, so I improvised as best I could. I smiled, and leaned my head down to give her some extra cheek/shoulder contact.

We talked for a few minutes; I was too nervous to remember what about. I'm not so good at conversing, and I admit to a few uncomfortable pauses this time. I'm certain she sensed the nervous energy pulsing through me, and I think I could feel some anticipation on her part as well. At each pause, her eyes seemed to be saying, "I'll bet you want to ask me something. Go ahead."

Maybe that was my imagination.

"Well, I better get going." A friend was waiting for her downstairs.

I knew I had to ask her right then, or prolong the conversation. I took the second option.

"Oh, you're going downstairs??"

"Yeah, are you? Need some help with the elevator?"

Something in me smiled. It worked. I could ask her in the elevator. It was quiet, and free of distractions.

The ride downstairs was quicker than I'd hoped, and far less romantic. The doors opened on the ground floor before I could even think of asking her. We slowly exited into the hallway. She paused, probably to say goodbye. Something in my brain decided to open the pressure valve, and the words escaped.

"Wouldyouwanna—" I caught my breath, and she smiled as if expecting me to ask a favor. "Catchamovieorsomething. Someti..umm, maybe next week?"

I wish I could read her reaction better. She blinked three times, and then fumbled a scrap of paper from her bag to write her number on. We both turned to the right, and walked together for a while.

The world doesn't feel as simple or as uninteresting to me as it did before. I've been home for over an hour now, and I'm still flying. It is a wonderful, free feeling. It's almost as if I broke out of a prison camp.

I feel like I made an accomplishment tonight, but I don't know what to thank for it: confidence; timing; destiny; pressure; loneliness. Which of these, if not all, were at work?

I'm not sure what will unfold, nor do I wish to speculate.

Poem for Janis Joplin

My eyes first fell upon you -
I remember a pair
of blueish sunglasses, askew,
and a girlish smile on a face
that seemed too small
to hold your secrets.

You grinned from your motorbike;
my head tilted like your shades.
I blinked. A giggling rose
danced in my mind.
I asked you for a ride. You smiled.
I was naïve. I wanted you to free me.

My eyes, at times, are like a woman's.
My body is a weak and tired man.
Here you are, though, holding me
and seeming more than human.
On stage in beads and stylish gowns,
you'd always beamed a radiance to me.
I don't think the others saw
the balance of you.
The female equally with male you sing.

On stage, a chord would bang a modern fury.
You'd howl as a raging princess,
your body, electric and furious,
full of a terrible memory, a secret
that gives you so much reason to scream,
and still you never scream. You touch
each blessed, cursed note and slip
across a line of song and warcry,
weaving intimacy with strength,
and becoming a menacing angel
to save us from who we weren't.
Warrior in beads,
bigger than the body trembling before
us, comes alive in you and shakes

violently our loneliness from us

and then, you relent,
your face returns to simple
smiles, insecure until you find
the character you need to be.

We lay together, and you look more than tired.
I knew you'd soon go on to stardom
if someone didn't stop you.
Looking at the pearls in your head
I knew it soon would be over.

I wanted to deliver you from Rock and Roll.
You'd saved me from suburbia,
taught me to be free,
yet you were never free.

What did it feel like?
Was it white-hot metal in your veins
(strong, for all of us)?
Was it pleasing, or was the high
in the return to life
like the sour candies I enjoy?
The pleasure comes when the pain goes away.

I'd look at you each day before you left
and wonder how I'd tell you that I knew
how hard life was, how amazing it felt
to take all of it straight and undiluted.
I'd step back, knowing I had no right
to speak without really knowing
the secret history of Rock and Roll.

There are many things
in our world which can
never be with you forever-
People,
Possessions,
And everyday emotion-

But the music doesn't abandon you.

Music born to embrace the soul
And soul born out of music.

It cradles us,
Embraces us,
Through all we'll ever need

It's in our heads-it blesses our minds
With trust for all that is to come;
To usher on the happiness,

Jazz grooves for us to borrow.
The Blues is with us when it's time
To rest amongst our sorrow.
The mighty songs of patriots
Put flaming glory in our heads.
Solemn dirges for repent
Light candles for the dead.

As the music man is laid to rest,
A sweet song fills the air.

May God smile on him.

Remember all the songs he sent;
for love
for fun
and for humanity.

[Dedicated to Frank Sinatra, and to the three generations of cats
who will never lose what he's given us...]